KT-484-922

Other titles in the series:
The Victim's Guide to the Doctor
The Victim's Guide to Middle Age
The Victim's Guide to the Dentist

Published in the USA in 1994 by Exley Giftbooks.
Published in Great Britain in 1994 by Exley Publications Ltd

Cartoons copyright © Roland Fiddy, 1994
Copyright © Exley Publications, 1994

ISBN 1-85015-430-9

A copy of the CIP data is available from the
British Library on request.

All rights reserved. No part of this publication may be
reproduced or transmitted in any form or by any means,
electronic or mechanical, including photocopy, recording or
any information storage and retrieval system without permission
in writing from the Publisher.

Printed in Spain by Grafo, S.A. – Bilbao.

Exley Publications Ltd, 16 Chalk Hill, Watford, Herts WD1 4BN,
United Kingdom.
Exley Giftbooks, 359 East Main Street, Suite 3D, Mount Kisco,
NY 10549, USA.

THE VICTIM'S GUIDE TO ...

Air Travel

THIS IS YOUR CAPTAIN PRAYING!

EXLEY

MT. KISCO, NEW YORK • WATFORD, UK

The excitement begins as soon as you enter the Airport .....

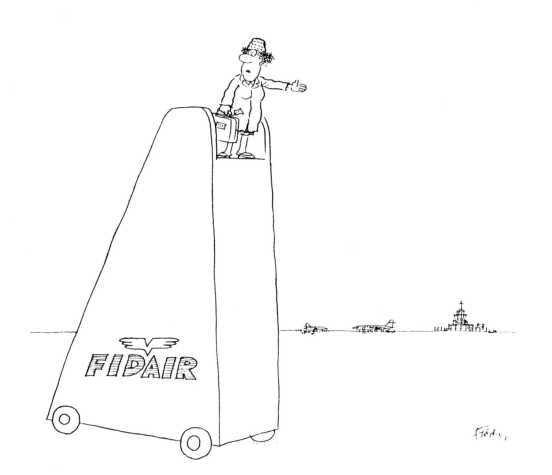

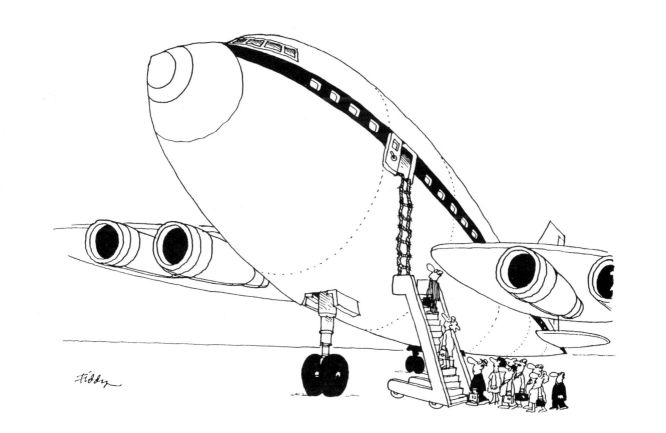

②

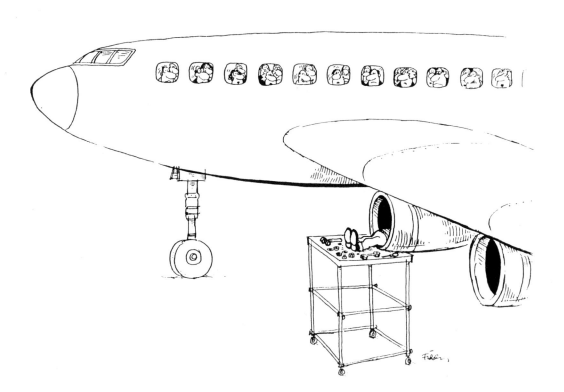

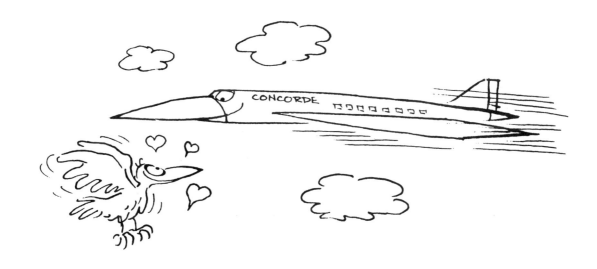

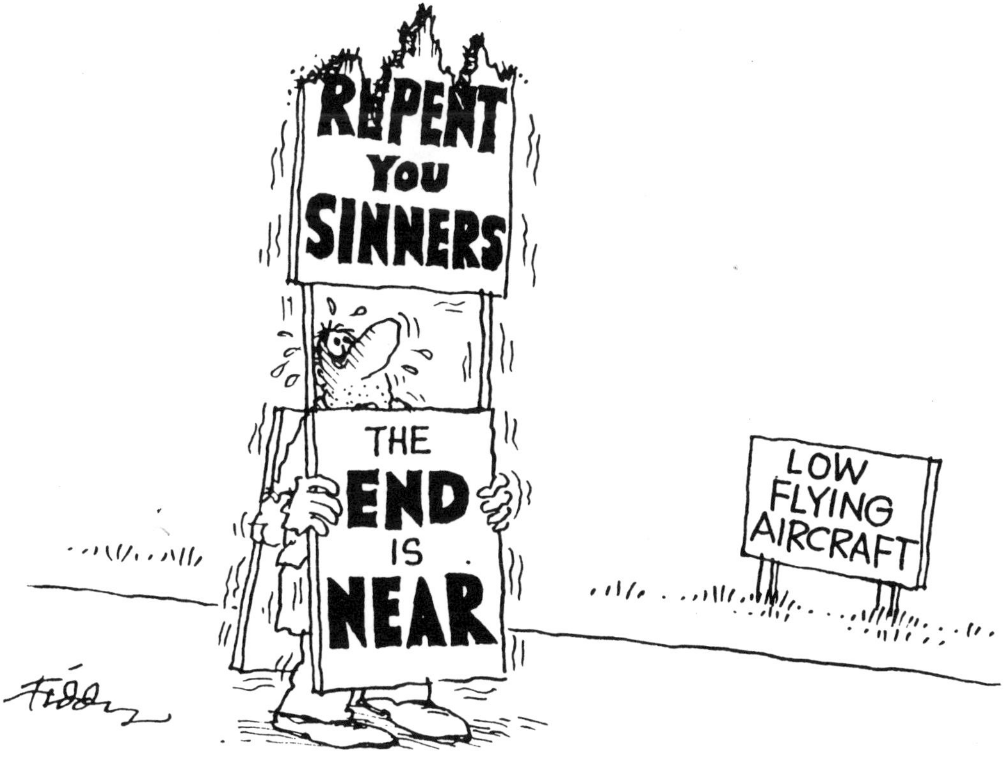
REPENT YOU SINNERS
THE END IS NEAR
LOW FLYING AIRCRAFT

PREPACKED PROBLEMS.

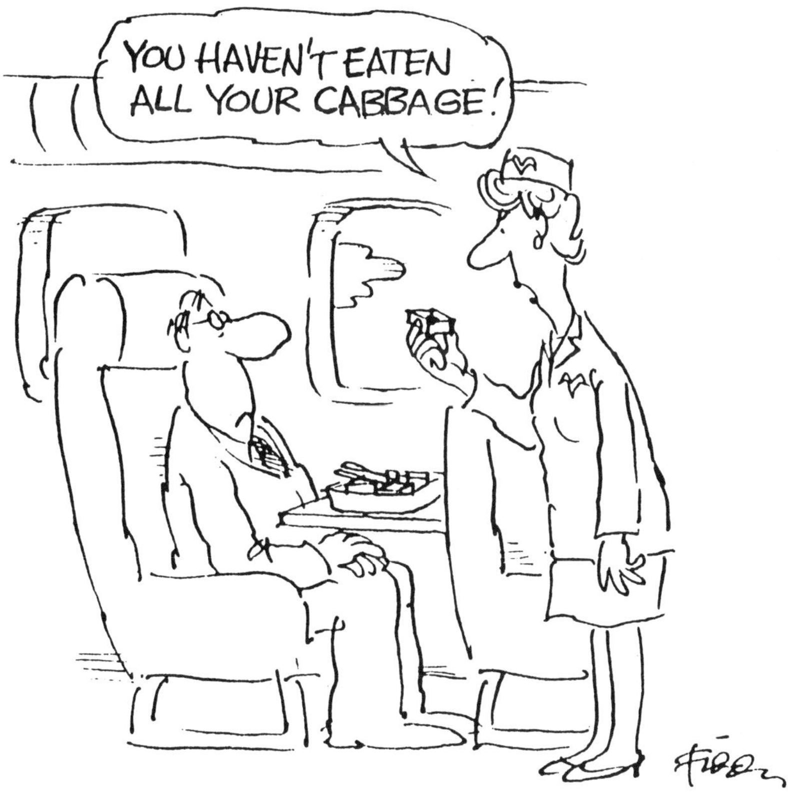
YOU HAVEN'T EATEN ALL YOUR CABBAGE!

THIS IS YOUR CAPTAIN SPEAKING, WITH A SPECIAL MESSAGE TO THOSE WHO ARE AFRAID OF FLYING. THIS IS NOTHING TO BE ASHAMED OF—BELIEVE ME, WE ARE **ALL** JUST AS NERVOUS AS YOU ARE....

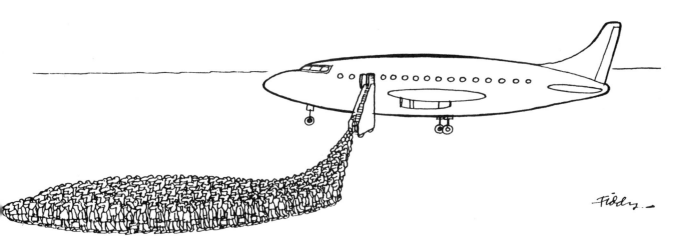

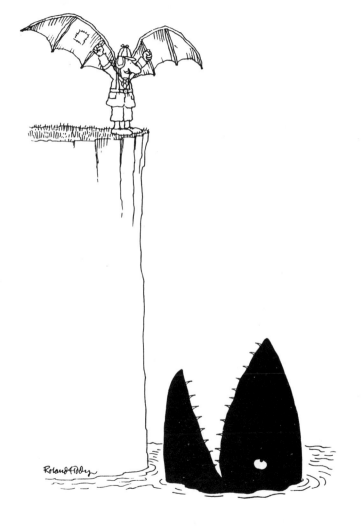

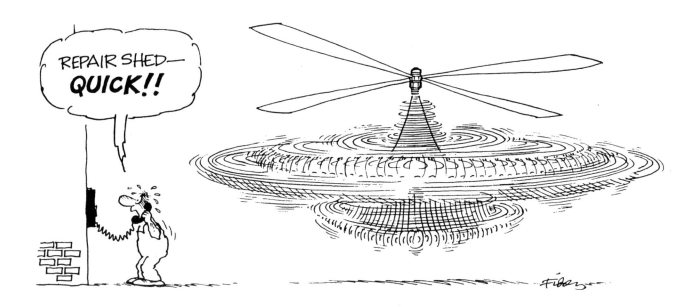

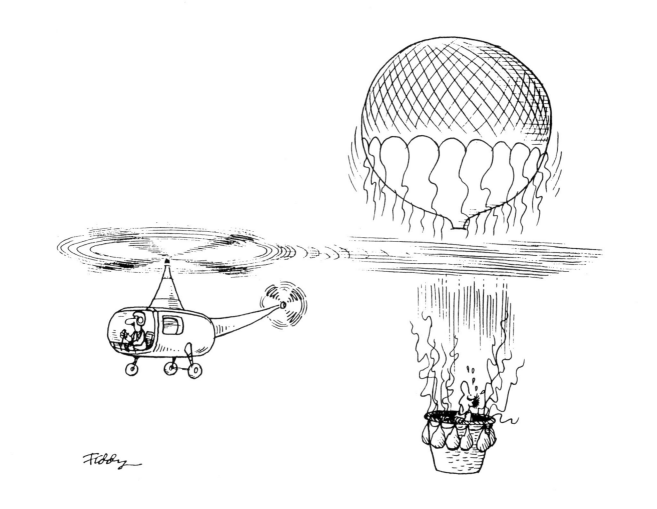

TODAY.

THE FUTURE

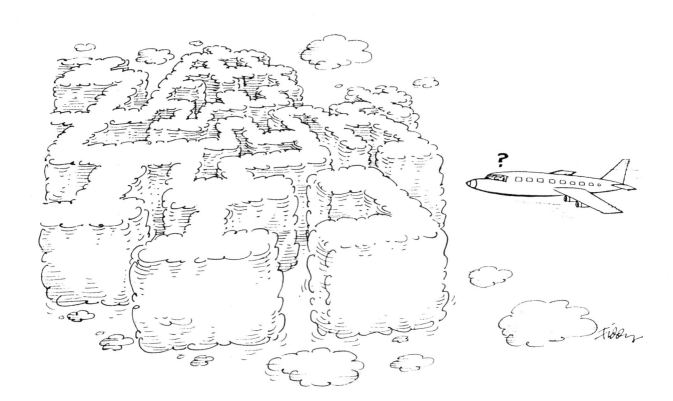

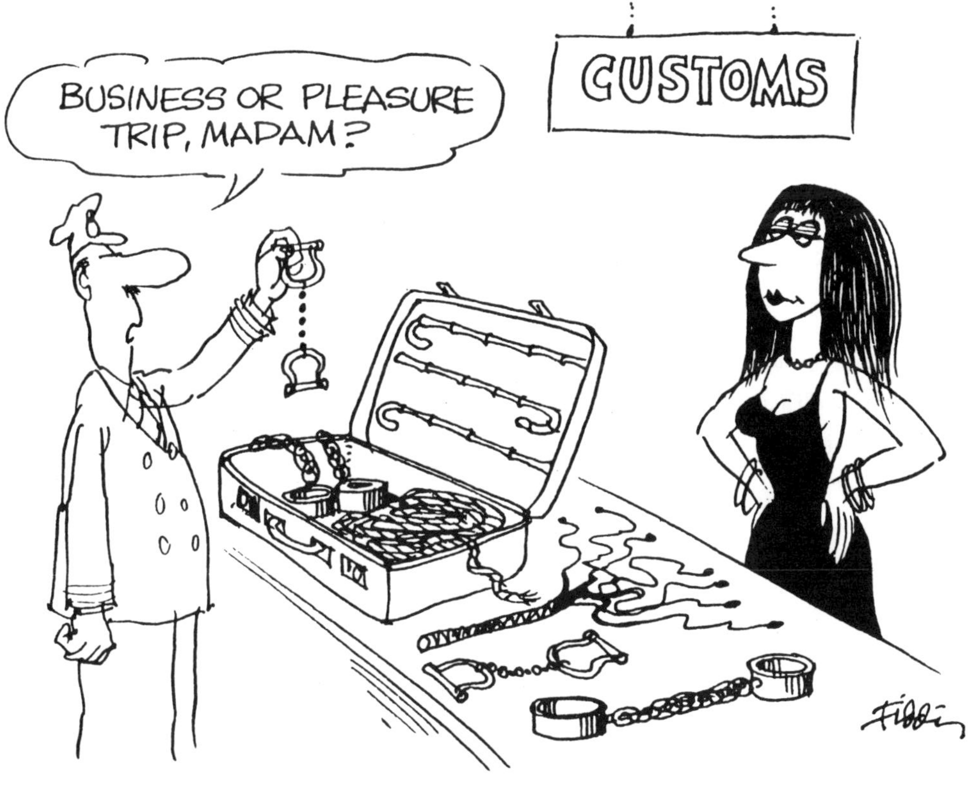
CUSTOMS
BUSINESS OR PLEASURE TRIP, MADAM?

Books in the "Victim's Guide" series
($4.99 £2.99 paperback)

Award winning cartoonist Roland Fiddy sees the funny side to life's phobias, nightmares and catastrophes.

The Victim's Guide to the Dentist
The Victim's Guide to the Doctor
The Victim's Guide to Middle Age
The Victim's Guide to Air Travel

Books in the "Fanatics" series
($4.99 £2.99 paperback)

The **Fanatic's Guides** are perfect presents for everyone with a hobby that has got out of hand. Eighty pages of hilarious black and white cartoons by Roland Fiddy.

The Fanatic's Guide to the Bed
The Fanatic's Guide to Cats
The Fanatic's Guide to Computers
The Fanatic's Guide to Dads
The Fanatic's Guide to Diets
The Fanatic's Guide to Dogs
The Fanatic's Guide to Golf
The Fanatic's Guide to Husbands
The Fanatic's Guide to Money
The Fanatic's Guide to Sex
The Fanatic's Guide to Skiing

Books in the "Crazy World" series
($4.99 £2.99 paperback)

The Crazy World of Aerobics (Bill Stott)
The Crazy World of Cats (Bill Stott)
The Crazy World of Cricket (Bill Stott)
The Crazy World of Gardening (Bill Stott)
The Crazy World of Golf (Mike Scott)
The Crazy World of the Greens (Barry Knowles)
The Crazy World of The Handyman (Roland Fiddy)
The Crazy World of Hospitals (Bill Stott)
The Crazy World of Housework (Bill Stott)
The Crazy World of Learning to Drive (Bill Stott)
The Crazy World of Love (Roland Fiddy)
The Crazy World of Marriage (Bill Stott)
The Crazy World of The Office (Bill Stott)
The Crazy World of Photography (Bill Stott)
The Crazy World of Rugby (Bill Stott)
The Crazy World of Sailing (Peter Rigby)
The Crazy World of Sex (David Pye)

Books in the "Mini Joke Book" series
($6.99 £3.99 hardback)

These attractive 64 page mini joke books are illustrated throughout by Bill Stott.

A Binge of Diet Jokes
A Bouquet of Wedding Jokes
A Feast of After Dinner Jokes
A Knockout of Sports Jokes
A Portfolio of Business Jokes
A Round of Golf Jokes
A Romp of Naughty Jokes
A Spread of Over-40s Jokes
A Tankful of Motoring Jokes

Great Britain: Order these super books from your local bookseller or From Exley Publications Ltd, 16 Chalk Hill, Watford, Herts WD1 4BN. (Please send £1.30 to cover post and packaging on 1 book, £2.60 on 2 or more books.)